The Whale House of the Chilkat

by

George T. Emmons

In the Time That Was

Done into English
by

J. Frederic Thorne

Printed on acid free ANSI archival quality paper.
ISBN: 978-1-78139-088-7
© 2012 Benediction Classics, Oxford.

Contents

The Whale House of the Chilkat 1
Preface 3
Introduction 5
The Old Whale House 15
Detail of the House Posts 21
Objects Associated With the House 28
The Present Whale House 30

In the Time That Was 35
The Water Carrier 49
Ta-ka the Mosquito and Khandatagoot the Woodpecker 57

The Whale House of the Chilkat

by

George T. Emmons

Preface

The material here presented has been gathered from the most reliable native sources throughout a period of twenty-five years of intimate personal acquaintance and association with the Tlingit, and treats of their past, before the exodus from their old villages to the mining camps and salmon canneries of the white man so reduced their numbers that communal life in the large old houses, upon which their social customs and practices depended, was rendered impossible, and the seed of a new life was sown.

I first visited the Chilkat in 1882, when little influenced by our civilization. They were a comparatively primitive people, living under their own well-established code of laws, subsisting on the natural products of the country, clothed in skins, furs, and trade blankets, practising ancestor worship in their elaborate ceremonial, cremating the dead, dominated by the superstitions of witchcraft and the practice of shamanism, proud, vain, sensitive, but withal, a healthy, honest, independent race, and friendly when fairly met.

Their villages then represented the best traditions of the past in both architecture and ornamentation. The houses of heavy hewn timbers, split from the giant spruces, were fortresses of defense, with narrow doorways for entrance and the smoke hole in the roof for light and ventilation.

But today this is all changed. The old houses have disappeared, the old customs are forgotten, the old people are fast passing, and with the education of the children and the gradual loss of the native tongue, there will be nothing left to connect them with the past. So on behalf of native history and my deep interest in the people, I offer this paper, describing in accurate detail one of the last relics of their culture. Had the Chilkat been able to work stone instead of wood, their country would now be the archaeological wonder of the Pacific Coast.

The illustrations in color are from sketches made upon the ground and are reasonably accurate both as to form and color. For their final form I am indebted to Mr. S. Ichikawa. To Winter and Pond I am under obligations for permission to use the photograph of the two Chilkat chiefs.

George T. Emmons.
Princeton, New Jersey,
April, 1916.

Introduction

Upon the discovery of the Northwest Coast of America, the Tlingit were found in possession of Southeastern Alaska with possibly the exception of the southernmost portion of Prince of Wales Island, which had been wrested from them by invading Haida from Masset on the Queen Charlotte Islands, during the latter half of the eighteenth century. From the testimony of the early explorers, this occupation seems to have been of sufficient age to have developed a racial type, speaking the same tongue, acknowledging established laws, and bound by like conventions. What knowledge we can gather of their origin and early life from their family traditions, songs, and geographical names, although fragmentary and vague, consistently tells of a uniform northward migration by water, along the coast and through the inland channels from the Tsimshian peninsula and Prince of Wales Island, which was constantly augmented by parties of Interior people descending the greater rivers to the sea.

An indefinite belief in an earlier coast population is current among the older people, and in confirmation of this, they refer to some family songs and local names still used but not understood. As the Tlingit are unquestionably a mixed race, this aboriginal element must have been absorbed and contributed its racial characteristics to the evolution of the present race.

The social organization of the Tlingit is founded on matriarchy and is dependent upon two exogamic parties, the members of which intermarry and supplement each other upon the many ceremonial occasions that mark their intercourse. The one claiming the Raven crest is known particularly among the northern Tlingit as Klar-de-nar, "one party," the other, more generally represented by the Wolf emblem has several names, local in character, referring to old living places, as

THE WHALE HOUSE OF THE CHILKAT

Shen-ku-ka-de, "belonging to Shenk," Sit-ka-de, "belonging to Sit," said to refer to the separation of the people after the flood when this branch settled at Sit, Gee-ya-de, etc. Outside of these there is one family claiming the Eagle crest that has no phratral standing, the members of which, as strangers, marry indiscriminately in either division, but in all cases the children belong to the mother's clan.

Fig. 1. Coudahwot and Yehlh-gouhu,
Chiefs of the Con-nuh-ta-di.

The two parties are subdivided into fifty-six existing consanguineal families or clans, and the names of some other's now extinct are remembered. Each of these, while retaining its phratral functions and privileges, is absolutely independent in government, succession, inheritance, and territory, and besides the phratral crest common to all, assumes others that are fully as prominent and often more in evidence. Within the family there is a well-defined aristocracy wholly dependent upon birth, from which the chiefs are chosen, an intermediate class consisting of those who have forced themselves to the front, through wealth, character, or artistic ability, and the poorer people. In earlier days there were many slaves who had no recognized rights.

Geographically considered, there are sixteen tribal divisions known as kwans, a contraction of ka (man) and an (land-lived on or claimed). These are purely accidental aggregations, with little cohesion, a grouping of one or more families of each phratry through migratory meeting or continual intermarriage, that live together in fixed villages for mutual protection and social advantages, but recognize no tribal head or authority, each family being a unit in itself. Very often the bitterest feuds existed between families within the tribe and of the same phratry, although if attacked by a stranger people all would unite for mutual protection.

Of these several tribes the Chilkat-kwan has been the most prominent since our acquaintance with Alaska. The relative importance of a primitive people measured by an abundant food supply, natural resources and geographic position as to favorable trade conditions was fully satisfied in their case. In their country about the head of Lynn Canal, with its two river systems flowing from lakes, the spawning beds of countless salmon furnished a nutritious and limitless staple food which was augmented by various other sea fish and seal in the inlets; bear, goat, and smaller mammals on the land; and exhaustless berry patches on the mountain sides. Their commanding position at the head of the inland channels controlling the mountain passes to the interior, gave them the monopoly of the fur trade of the upper Yukon Valley, and the placer copper fields of the White River region. These products, unknown to the coastal area, were economically important in primitive days, and after the advent of Europeans the increased demand for furs, and their greater value, made this trade even more lucrative. That they fully realized its value is demonstrated by their determination to retain control of it, for when the Hudson's Bay Company established the factory of Fort Selkirk at the mouth of the Pelly

River in 1852, a war party under the celebrated Chief Chartrich, trailed in some three hundred miles, surprised, captured, and burned the post, and warned the occupants against any further encroachment upon their established zone of trade, and they continued to enjoy these rights until the discovery of the Klondike gold fields, when the influx of whites over-ran the country and destroyed their industries.

The earliest mention of this people occurs in a report of the Russian Pilot Ismaïlof who, when visiting Yakutat in 1788, notes the presence of a large body of Chilkat. In 1794 a boat expedition from Vancouver's vessels, while exploring the head of Lynn Canal, met with a hostile reception from a considerable number of natives and only averted trouble by a hasty retreat. Lieutenant Whitby, the commander of the party, was told of eight chiefs of great consequence who had their homes on and about the Chilkat River, indicating an extensive population.

Fig. 2. An Old House, Kluckwan.

Under the Russian régime, beyond the mere claim of sovereignty, no jurisdiction was exercised over this people except the distribution of national flags and Imperial medals. All trading was guardedly carried on from the decks of armed vessels, and long after the American occupation they were permitted to live unmolested, until their country became the highway of travel to the interior.

The Tlingit were a canoe people and might be termed semi-nomadic, as they were on their hunting grounds in the early spring and late fall, while the summer season was spent in the fishing camps by the salmon streams, but notwithstanding these long absences they built substantial villages where, except for social activities, they spent the winter in comparative idleness.

Fig. 3. Con-nuh-ta-di Grave Houses, Kluckwan.

As they looked to the sea for their principal food supply, their villages were directly on the shore just above the high water mark, in sheltered coves where they could land and launch their canoes in any weather and at any stage of the tide. But the Chilkat, differing from all of the other Tlingit, lived just beyond the open water, in a rather restricted territory, on rivers that were veritable storehouses of food, bringing their abundance of fish life to their very doors, and so permitting them to remain at home throughout the year, except when on their trading trips to the interior, which gave their habitations a more permanent character, and contributed to the unity of communal life.

Of the four principal old villages, all of which have survived the ravages of constant strife and the still more deadly by-products of civilization—liquor and disease—Kluckwan (mother town) has always held the first place in size, wealth, and the character of its people. It retained its supremacy long after the larger of the more southern coast villages had gone to decay, as its more interior and isolated position and the independent and aggressive reputation of its population kept white traders at a distance. The discovery of gold near Juneau and the establishment of the several salmon canneries at the mouth of the river drew away its people, and communal life in the large old houses, that was dependent upon the united efforts of the whole household was made impossible by the absence of many, and the want of coöperation of others who elected to live by themselves. With the introduction of schools and the efforts of missionaries to break up the old customs, the village has undergone a complete change and the old houses have disappeared or have been modernized.

The village lies at the edge of a gradual slope on the north bank of the Chilkat, twenty miles from its mouth, where the swift current concentrated in a single channel forms a strong eddy that permits the landing of canoes at any stage of the river. The houses in a single and double row follow the trend of the shore for upwards of three-quarters of a mile, but far enough back to allow for the smoke houses, fish drying frames, and canoe shelters, and in the rear are the grave houses (Fig. 3) and the now disused cremation grounds strewn with charred logs and partly burnt funeral pyres. Just beyond the village at either end, in the cottonwood groves, hidden in the underbrush and covered with moss, are the crumbling remains of the shaman's dead houses, guarded by elaborately carved spirit figures and decayed canoes.

The houses of each of the four resident totemic families are grouped about that of the chief for mutual protection, giving the appearance of three separate villages, as the two centrally located families through increase of numbers, have been brought into closer union. In each group the houses of the aristocracy and those of the poorer classes are of like construction, differing however in size, strength of material, interior appointments, and ornamentation.

Of the five totemic families that form the Chilkat-kwan, not including a sixth subdivision, four are resident here, while individuals of the others through intermarriage are scattered through the village but without house standing. The traditions of all of these speak of a migration from the southern border northward through the inland channels.

The Wolf phratry is represented by three families: the Kágwantān, Tuck-este-nar, and Duck-clar-way-di. The first two are closely related and claim to be offshoots of a parent stock and to have migrated north from the coast between the mouths of the Nass and the Skeena rivers and in earlier times they lived inland on these rivers. The last-named is unquestionably of interior origin and it is possible that all three are of like ancestry.

The sole representative of the Raven party is the Kon-nuh-ta-di with which this paper deals. Their legendary history, so imaginary and interesting, is closely associated with the wanderings and antics of "Yehlh," the Raven creator, while the earliest family traditions are centered about the south and west coast of the Prince of Wales and contiguous islands. There is a hazy belief in the minds of the older people, handed down through generations, that in the earliest days there came to these shores from seaward, a people of unknown origin who landed and lived on Dall Island, and later spread along the southern coast of Prince of Wales Island. The descendants of one of the two original women, represented as sisters, later crossed Dixon Entrance and peopled the Queen Charlotte Islands, founding the Haida, while those who remained, uniting with migratory bands from the Interior were the progenitors of the Tlingit.

The three principal families forming the Tanta-kwan that lived thereabouts in the eighteenth century, until expelled by the Haida invasion from Masset, and then crossed over to the mainland where they are still found, are the Ta-qway-di, Kik-sat-di, and Kon-nuh-hut-di, all of which have formed factors of great importance in peopling the coast of Alaska as far north as Comptroller Bay, and are still represented in all of the more important Tlingit tribes. The tribal name Tanta, was taken from their country, the Prince of Wales Island, Tan, "Sealion" so named from the abundance of this animal on the seaward coast. The Kon-nuh-hut-di are said to have removed, at some early day, to Port Stewart within the mainland entrance of Beam Canal, which they called "Con-nuh," (safe, sheltered) and from which they derived their family name (people of, or belonging to, Con-huh), but finding the climate more severe than that of the islands, and with no compensating advantages of food, they returned to their former home. A slight variation of the name Kon-nuh-ta-di which is not accounted for, distinguishes the Chilkat and more northern branches of the family from the Tanta and Taku. Another name seldom used, but very pretentious and tribal in character, is Shuck-ka-kwan "highest or first-man tribe" or Shuck-ka-kon-nuh-ta-di, claiming superiority through a relationship with Yehlh, in reference to his struggle with Gun-nook, the supernatural keeper of fresh water, when in his efforts to escape through the smoke hole of the house with what he had stolen he was caught and held fast until he was smoked black.

THE WHALE HOUSE OF THE CHILKAT

At a very early period they must have lived on the central west coast of Prince of Wales Island, near Klawak, in a village or country called Tuck-anee "outside town" where the people were known locally as Tuckanadi "outside town people" as the scene of one of their principal hero tales is laid hereabouts (the struggle of Duck-toolh with the sealions) which it is claimed was the cause of one of the northward migrations of a body of the family. It was certainly after this happening, and possibly connected with it, that a considerable party separated and traveled north through the inland channels to the head of tidewater, and then up the Chilkat River until they reached the site of Kluckwan where they finally settled and have ever since remained. This movement must date back many years, for the Russian Pilot Ismaïlof, as previously noted, in visiting Yakutat in 1888 met "a chief Ilk-hak with a large force of one hundred warriors who had journeyed up the coast from their winter home on the Chilkat River to trade."

Ilk-hak or Yehlh-kok "Raven fragrance or smell" is an hereditary name belonging strictly to the Kon-nuh-ta-di family (and as a coincidence it happens to be that of the present chief to whom I am indebted for certain information herein contained), and to have extended their commercial activities to such a distance and with such a numerous retinue would bespeak a considerable age and settled state in their new home.

Other migrations northward are known to have occurred at later periods; One party following the outside coast settled in a bay above Cape Spencer where much glacial ice collected and they took the name Tih-ka-di (people of or belonging to the icebergs) but of these none remain.

Another body, taking a more easterly course among the islands, stopped at Chyeek on the Chatham Straits shore of Admiralty Island with the Hootz-ah-tar-kwan, but trouble with the Dasheton clan arose over a woman and they removed in a body to Stevens Passage and joined the Taku-kwan of which they form an integral part today under the original name Kon-nuh-hut-di.

In the latter portion of the eighteenth century, the Tanta-kwan including this family, was driven out of the southern portion of the Prince of Wales Island by the Haida and crossing Clarence Straits settled on Annette and adjacent islands. Their principal village was Tark-an-ee (winter town) at Port Chester where New Metlakatla now stands, and was a very large settlement, a totem pole village, as the decayed remains showed thirty years ago. In war with the Stickheen, this village was destroyed and also a later one across the island, Chake-an-ee (Thimble berry town) at Port Tamgass, when they crossed to Cat Island and then to the mainland and made a last stand at Tongass where they remained until the founding of Saxman and Ketchikan.

None of this family is found today on Prince of Wales Island, their original home. The principal branch lives at Chilkat where they have always been accorded the highest place with the Ka-gwan-tan, with whom they have so intermarried through generations, that it often happens that the chiefs of each family are father and son.

The personal names more frequently refer to the Raven, their most honored crest, as they claim to be the first family of this phratry, and it is the more conspicuously displayed on the totemic headdress and ceremonial paraphernalia. They claim and use a great many other emblems as the whale, frog, wood-worm, silver salmon, hawk, owl, moon, starfish, and in their house carvings and painting they illustrate the hero deeds and conquests of their ancestors in their early struggles with mythical animals and supernatural beings.

Facial painting played an important rôle in Tlingit life. The several pigments differently applied in various characters depended upon the purpose and the occasion. As a protection against snowblindness, the glare of the sunshine on the water, the bite of insects and as a cosmetic to preserve and whiten the complexion, a hemlock fungus was charred, powdered, and applied to the face, which had previously been covered with a mixture of melted suet and spruce gum, to which it adhered and hardened, forming a red-black covering impervious to water.

For mourning and anger the face was blackened with charcoal.

When on war parties, the painting was in red or black or both, in fanciful and hideous characters, but if suddenly surprised, they would grab a piece of charcoal from the fire and rub it over the face to disguise their personality and hide any expression of fear.

The most elaborate painting was used in the winter ceremonials and dances. The designs were almost entirely totemic in character even when improvised for the occasion and apparently expressionless. They were either geometric and symbolic in figure, or represented the animal form in profile or some characteristic feature which distinguished it. In the latter case the figure was stamped on the cheek or forehead with a wood die. The primitive colors were black, from powdered charcoal, and red, from pulverized ocher, but after the advent of Europeans, vermilion of commerce took the place of the duller mineral red. Yellow, white, and greenish blue were occasionally used, more particularly by the southern tribes, but seldom, if ever, by the Chilkat.

The most important painting of the face was that of the dead when placed in state awaiting cremation, and this represented the crest of the phratry rather than one of the assumed emblems of the family or subdivisions. Most all of the Raven party, certainly all of the older and more important families, and particularly the Kon-nuh-ta-di used Yehlh-thluou, "Raven's nose," in the form of an isosceles triangle, in black, the apex at the bridge of the nose, the sides enclosing the nose and mouth, the base extending across the chin. This painting seems to have been the right of all of the Raven families and was almost universally used by them, although minor crest figures were sometimes employed, as the Kon-nuh-hut-di of the Southern tribes are said to have painted the starfish figure although I have never seen it so used, although it was a festival decoration.

It was an old custom, but rather a privilege claimed by the chiefs and house masters of the aristocracy, to give names to the communal houses upon the occasion of their dedication, after the walls were up and the roof was on, when those of the opposite phratry who had assisted in the construction were feasted and compensated. Of course, in the evolution of society, men of strong character, successful in war, with wealth and many followers would compel such recognition as would permit them to found a house and give it a name, but in order to do so, the potlatch would have to be of undue proportion. The strongest characteristics of the Tlingit are pride, vanity, and a dread of ridicule, so unless one was absolutely assured of more than a formal acceptance of the act by both his own and the other tribal families he would hesitate to place himself in a false position, subject to criticism. The highest and most honored names thus given, were those of the totemic emblem, or referring to some particular feature of the crest figure, as "Raven house," "Brown bear house," "Eagle nest house," "Killer-whale dorsal fin house," etc. Other names meaning less were those of position, shape, material, etc., as "Point house," "Box house", "Bark house," "Drum house," "Big house," "Lookout house," etc. In any case a name once given survived the mere structure. It was a dedication of the site and without any further ceremony belonged to all future houses built thereon.

The Old Whale House

When I first visited Kluckwan in 1885, the large old communal houses of the Kon-nuh-ta-di were still standing, the principal one of which, that of the hereditary chief, Yough-hit, "Whale house," was in the last stages of decay and uninhabitable, although the interior fittings were intact and it was still used upon festival occasions. It was unquestionably the most widely known and elaborately ornamented house, not only at Chilkat, but in Alaska. It occupied the site of much older houses and it is claimed much larger ones. It is said to have been built by Kate-tsu about or prior to 1835 and stood in the middle of the village. It represented the best type of Tlingit architecture, a broad low structure of heavy hewn spruce timbers, with noticeably high corner posts, that gave it a degree of character wholly wanting in the larger houses of the Vancouver Island people. It faced the river with a frontage of 49 feet 10 inches and a depth of 53 feet which was approximately the proportions of Tlingit houses large and small. The four broad, neatly finished corner posts, and the intermediate ones on the sides and back were mortised in length, to receive the ends of the wall planks of spruce or hemlock that were laid horizontally along the sides and back, while the front was formed by two heavy bed pieces placed one above the other extending across the front, dove-tailed into the corner posts, and reaching to the height of the door sill, cut out along the upper edge to receive the lower ends of the broad vertical planks that extend to the roof, and fitted under corresponding grooves in the cornice cappings that in the rear of the corner posts were notched and grooved to fit in the post. It will thus be seen that the old houses formed a solid structure, the frame and planking supporting each other without the use of spikes. The doorway, that was the only opening in the walls, was approached by two steps over three feet above the ground, it was narrow and low as a defensive measure, so that but one could enter at a time, and then only in a stooping posture equally impossible for attack or defense. The roof covering consisted of a confusion of overlapping spruce boards and slabs of bark that originally had been held down by smaller tree trunks extending the depth of the structure and held in place by heavy boulders at the ends. The smoke hole in the center of the roof which both lighted and ventilated the interior had been protected by a movable shutter balanced on a cross bar resting on two supports so that it could be shifted to either side as desired.

Fig. 4. The Whale House of the Chilkat.

The interior formed an excavation four feet nine inches below the ground level, with two receding step-like platforms. The lower square floor space 26 feet by 26 feet 9 inches, constituted the general living and working room common to all, except that portion in the rear and opposite the entrance, which was reserved for the use of the house chief, his immediate family and most distinguished guests. This was the place of honor in all Tlingit houses upon all occasions, ceremonial or otherwise. The flooring of heavy, split, smoothed planks of varying widths extended around a central gravelled fireplace six feet by six feet and a half, where all of the cooking was done, over a wood fire which also heated the house in winter. In front of and a little to the right of the fire space entered by a small trap door in the floor barely large enough to admit a person, was a small cellar-like apartment used as a steam bath, by heating boulders in the nearby fire, dropping them on the floor below with split wood tongs, and pouring water upon them to generate the vapor when the bather entered and the opening was covered over.

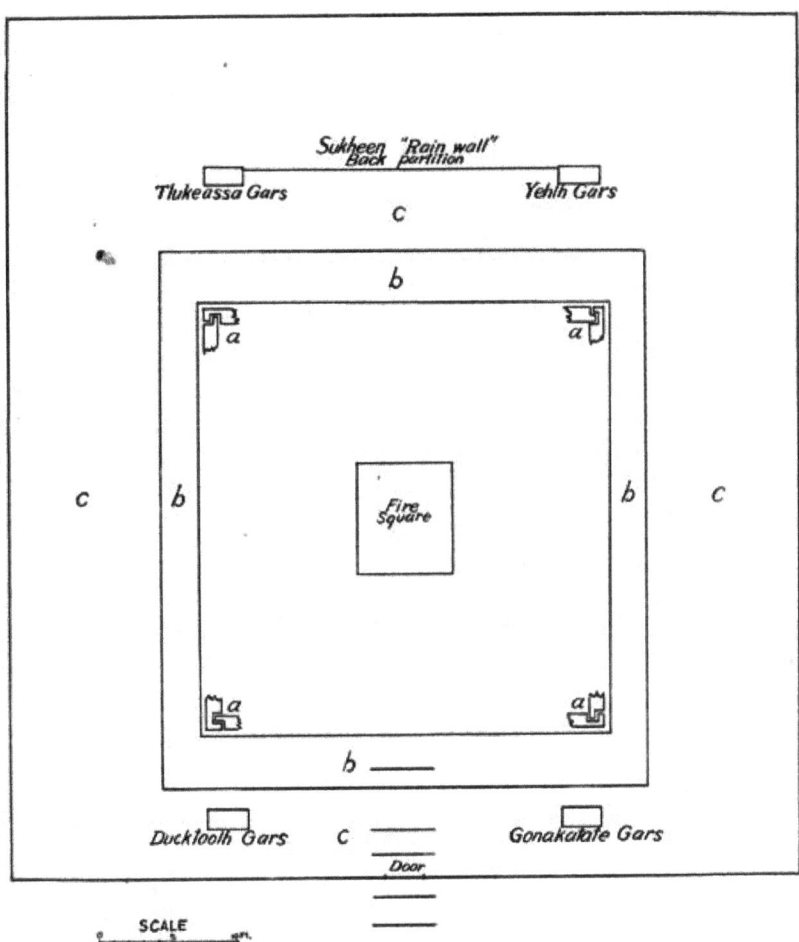

Fig. 5. Groundplan of the Whale House. In size, it was 49 ft. 10 in. front by 53 ft. deep. From a plan drawn by the author.

The first platform extending around the main floor at an elevation of 2¾ feet, comparatively narrow, with a width of 2½ feet along the sides, and slightly more at the ends, served both as a step, and a lounging place in the daytime, and that in front, broken by the steps descending from the doorway, was utilized for firewood, fresh game, fish, water baskets, and such larger household articles and implements as were in general use. The retaining walls of this platform consisted of four heavy hewn spruce timbers approximately 27 feet long, 3 feet wide, and 5 inches thick, and so fitted with mortise and tenon at opposite ends that they supported each other without artificial fastenings. The faces of these timbers were beautifully finished in the finest adze work, and those on either side and at the back were carved in low relief to represent a remarkable extended figure, neither wholly human nor animal, with widely outstretched arms and legs, painted in red. It may be that the artist conceived and executed this form merely as a decorative feature, without meaning, or if it was his purpose to present a recognizable figure he followed that characteristic and well established privilege of native art in exaggeration to make the subject conform to the decorative field. The old chief, Yehlh-guou, "Raven's slave," said that the figure symbolized "Kee-war-kow" the highest heaven where those who were killed in war and died violent deaths went, and are seen at play in the Aurora Borealis. Another explanation is that it merely represented a man warming himself before the central fire. (Plate 1.)

The upper and broader platform, rising two feet above that below, was at the ground level, and was floored with heavy planks. It had a depth of ten feet on the sides which was greatly increased at the back and correspondingly diminished in front. The four heavy retaining timbers forming the walls and supporting the platform were thirty-one feet at the front and back and thirty-three feet along the sides, two feet wide, and five inches in thickness, and were fitted together at the ends as previously described, and shown in the house plan. On the carefully adzed face carved in low relief, equidistant from the corners and from each other, arranged in echelon, were three representations of the "tinneh" the ceremonial copper and in connection with this it may be noted that one of the names of the house chief was Tinneh-sarta "Keeper of the copper." This platform constituted the sleeping place of the inmates. Each family occupied a certain space according to number and relative importance, the poorer members being nearer the door. The spaces were separated from each other by walls of chests, baskets, and bundles containing the family wealth in skins, blankets, clothing, ceremonial paraphernalia, and food products. On the walls were hung weapons, traps, snares, and hunting gear. Cedarbark mats covered the floor over which was laid the bedding consisting of pelts of the caribou, mountain sheep, goat, and bear, and blankets of lynx, fox, and squirrel, which in the daytime were ordinarily rolled up for economy of space. Sometimes these chambers were partly enclosed by skins or old canoe sails. The back compartment occupying the space between the two rear interior posts was partitioned off by a very beautiful carved wood screen which will be described later. This was the chamber of the chief and his immediate family. (Plate 2)

At the level of this upper platform, firmly imbedded in the ground equidistant from the sides and nearer the front than the back wall, were four vertical elaborately carved posts "gars" nine feet three inches high and two feet six inches wide, which supported the roof structure. The heads were hollowed to receive two neatly rounded tree trunks almost two feet in diameter extending from front to rear, on top of these at intervals were placed heavy cross bars which in turn supported two smaller rounded longitudinal beams placed that distance towards the center that would give the necessary pitch to the roof, lighter cross pieces spanned these, on which rested the ridge pole in two sections to allow for the smoke hole.

The private apartment of the house chief occupied the central portion of the upper rear platform, and was partitioned off in front, by a screen of thin native-split red cedar planks of varying widths, neatly fitted vertically, and sewed together with withes of spruce root, countersunk, to make it appear a solid piece. It extended between the two rear carved posts that supported the roof structure, and was twenty feet long by nine and a half feet high. The front surface was smoothed with dogfish skin or equisetum, and elaborately carved in low relief and painted to represent the rain spirit, which was symbolized by the great central figure with outstretched arms, while the small crouching figures in the border around the sides and top known as Su-con-nutchee "raindrops splash up," represented the splash of the falling drops after striking the ground. The whole partition was called Su-kheen "rain wall."

The round hole through the body, over which was formerly hung a dressed caribou or goatskin, formed the entrance to the chamber, which received its only light and ventilation over the top of the screen from the smoke hole in the roof. There seems to be a difference of opinion today as to who executed this work. Yehlh-kok the present chief of the family says that it was done by Kate-tsu, the chief who built the house, and that the painting was the work of Skeet-lah-ka, a later chief and an artist of wide repute, the father of Chartrich, who in 1834 just prior to the lease of the littoral by the Russian Government to the Hudson's Bay Company, accompanied the first Russians who

THE WHALE HOUSE OF THE CHILKAT

ascended the Chilkat River, which would carry it well back in the early portion of the last century which was the Victorian age of Northwest Coast art.

Others, while agreeing as to the painting, claim that the carving was designed and executed by a Tsimshian. But whether the work of the former or the latter, the conventionalized design, and particularly the multiplicity of small figures around the principal one is essentially Tsimshian in character and entirely different from the realism of Tlingit art.

It is unquestionably the finest example of native art, either Tlingit or Tsimshian, in Alaska, in boldness of conception,—although highly conventionalized in form,—in execution of detail, and in the selection and arrangement of colors.

The four interior posts "gars" on which rest the heavy longitudinal beams that support the roof structure are elaborately carved in high relief, a commingling of human and animal forms. Each one illustrates some hero tale or important incident in the early life of the family, or a tradition of the wanderings and antics of Yehlh, "the Raven" with whom they claim a certain relationship. Each post is named from the story told. They are of red cedar, brought from the south, and were carved by a Tsimshian who also carved the figures on the faces of the retaining timbers of the first platform. For all of this work he received in payment ten slaves, fifty dressed moose-skins, and a number of blankets.

Besides these there were four other posts known as Teetle-Gars "Dog salmon post." They presented a slightly rounded surface, carved in low relief, painted in dull colors, inlaid with opercula and representing, as the name indicated, the dog salmon. They were much decayed and only two were standing at the height of the upper platform at the sides in 1885. They had been used originally as interior posts in some house but had passed their period of usefulness and were preserved simply as relics of the past.

Detail of the House Posts

Gonakatate-Gars

The carved interior post to the right of the doorway entering was known as Gonakatate-Gars and told a story of Yehlh, the Raven. (Plate 3a.)

Gonakatate was believed to be a great sea monster, half animal and half fish, variously represented according to the imagination of the artist, but generally shown with fore feet, a characteristic dorsal fin, and the tail of a fish, but again it is said that in rising from the water it appeared as a beautifully ornamented house front. It brought great good fortune to one who saw it.

The principal figure extending from near the top to the bottom with front and hind paws represents this monster holding a whale by the flipper with the tail in its mouth and the head between the hind feet, for the Gonakatate is believed to capture and eat whales. The figure of a woman on the back of the whale is called Stah-ka-dee-Shawut which is an older name of the Qwash-qwa-kwan, a family that came from the interior and settled on the coast about Yakutat, and as the scene of this adventure is placed thereabouts and with the matriarchal system the woman would indicate the family. The use of her figure would serve to mark the locality which is the only explanation for her appearance.

In the blow hole of the whale is the head of the Raven which is the significant feature of the whole carving that illustrates the story. The smaller head at the top, ornamented with human hair is called Go-nakatate-Yuttee, "Gonakatate's child," that holds the head of the hawk in its paws. While the hawk is an emblem of the family, these figures are merely ornamental and have no connection with the story.

The story of the Gonakatate-Gars is as follows:—

During the wanderings of Yehlh "Raven" along the coast of Alaska above the mouth of the Alsech River, he saw a whale blowing, far out to sea, and being always hungry he greatly wanted to capture it, but he had neither spear nor line and only his fire bag of flint, stone, and tinder. He thought that he might kill the whale if he could only get inside, so when it came up to breathe he flew in the blow hole and reaching the stomach, struck a light, and made a fire that soon killed it.

When it floated inshore and was rolled on the beach by the breakers, he tried to escape as he had entered, but the blow hole had partly closed and he could only get his head out. He saw a young man coming down to the shore and he commenced to sing in a loud voice. This greatly surprised him and he hastened back to the camp to tell the old people that there was strange singing in a stranded whale, which brought all the villagers to the scene, and they proceeded to cut open the whale at the blow hole when the Raven flew out singing khoonee, khoonee, "cleaned out the blow hole." When the people had cut up the whale and tried out the blubber into grease the Raven returned in human form, and asked them how they got the whale, and if they had heard singing within, for he told them that long ago this had happened in his country, and all of those who ate the grease had died. This so frightened the people that they left the grease boxes on the shore and returned to the village, when the Raven sat down and ate all the grease they had prepared.

Duck-Toolh-Gars

The carved interior post, to the left of the doorway entering, was named Duck-toolh-Gars, and illustrates a hero tale of the family that occurred before their northern migration. The human figure represents Duck-toolh "Black-skin" (typifying strength), tearing the sealion in two. The head at the base symbolizes the rock island on which the sealion hauled, when this incident took place. The head of Duck-toolh is wrapped around with sealion intestines and is ornamented with human hair hanging down over the face. The sealion forms the central figure; the protruding tongue indicates death, as the body is split in half. The fore flippers are parallel with the body under the man's forearms and the back flippers rest on his shoulders.

It is said that in the early life of the Kon-nuh-hut-di, before their migration north, when they lived on the west coast of Prince of Wales Island, at or near the present site of Klawak, at Tuck-anee "just by the outside" from which the inhabitants took the local name Tuck-an-a-di "outside country people" from their home on the ocean coast, there was a young man, the nephew of the chief, named Duck-toolh "Blackskin," but nicknamed At-kaharsee "nasty man" from his generally dirty condition.

The villagers depended largely upon the flesh of the sealion for food, its hide was used for armor and other economic purposes while the whisker bristles were greatly prized for the crown of the ceremonial headdress.

These animals were found in great numbers on a rocky island far to seaward (supposed to have been Foresters Island), but the ocean passage in their frail canoes was very dangerous and with their primitive spears and clubs it took courage and strength to succeed in the hunt, and so they prepared themselves for the undertaking by much exercise, and hardened their bodies by sea bathing in the early morning throughout the winter. But Duck-Toolh seemingly practised none of these things, he slept late and although of great size was looked upon as lazy and weak until he became the laughing stock even of the children. In the household was a powerful man named Kash-ka-di, who in passing for his morning plunge would kick Duck-toolh and call him by his nickname, which he never resented. Upon coming out of the water each morning the bathers would test their strength by trying to pull up and break smaller trees. All of this time Duck-toolh was shamming, for every night after all had gone to sleep he would steal out and sit in the ice cold water by the hour, and coming out would beat himself with bundles of brush to keep up his circulation, then he would enter the house and throwing a little water on the hot coals to make steam, and wrapping himself in his bark mat would lie down and go to sleep in the ashes which covered his body and gave him his nickname. One night while he was sitting in the water he heard a whistle, and saw a heavily built man rise out of the sea. He came to him and told him to get up, when he whipped him on the back four times and with each stroke he fell down. Then he gave Duck-toolh the sticks and told him to whip him, which had no effect upon him and he said, "You have not gained strength yet." This operation was again repeated which gave Duck-toolh great strength, and then they wrestled with each other, but neither could throw the other. The strange man said, "Now you are very powerful I have given you my strength," when a heavy fog suddenly drove in from the sea and enveloped him and he disappeared. Then Duck-toolh ran about and broke the limbs off the trees with little effort, but he put them together again and they froze in place for he did not want any one to know that strength had come to him. He felt very happy, and was very willing to do anything for any one or to accept the ridicule and abuse heaped upon him. In the morning, Kash-ka-di, after coming out of the water, ran about trying his strength and he took the great limb that was stuck together in his hands and pulled it apart. He boasted to everyone that strength had come to him and that he was ready now to go out against the sealion. Duck-toolh said, "Yes, he would go too," which made every one laugh. Even the girls made fun of him and asked him what he could do, for he was like them, and he said that he could bail the canoe, which was a woman's or child's work. He washed and put on clean clothes and going to his grandmother said, "You have no tlhan," (strips of fur woven into blankets); "you have no da" (martin skin). She answered, "Yes" and gave him a strip of fur with which he tied up his front hair, taken in a bunch (this was done when one felt angry), and he dabbed his mouth with red paint, but still the people laughed at him, although he looked like a chief. Then the canoe started for the sealion grounds and while Kash-ka-di boasted of his great strength and what he would do, Duck-toolh sat silently in the bottom of the canoe. When they reached the rocks Kash-ka-di jumped out and grabbing a great sealion by its hind flippers tried to tear it in two, but he was thrown high in the air and killed on the rocks. Then Duck-toolh laughed and said, "Who broke the tree," "I break it," and he jumped on the rock and grabbed the sealion and tore it apart, beat the brains out of the smaller ones, and for some unknown reason he wound the intestines of the animals around his head. Then they loaded the canoe with the carcasses and returned home and everyone knew that Duck-toolh was strength and he became a very powerful and wealthy man. Some versions of this story say that he remained alone on the island for some time during which the spirit of the doctor came to him, but my informant knew nothing of this.

Yehlh-Gars

The carved post on the right of the ornamental screen was named Yehlh-Gars "Raven Post," and told the story of the capture of Ta "the king salmon." The main figure shows the Raven in human form holding a head with a projecting blade-like tongue, which is known as Tsu-hootar "jade adze." At the bottom is the head of a fish which should have been that of the king salmon, but through a mistake of the carver it resembles more nearly that of the sculpin. Coming out of the mouth of the Raven is a bird form called Tu-kwut-lah-Yehlh, "telling lies raven," which symbolizes the lies the Raven told to the little birds mentioned in the story. (Plate 4a.)

Many of the myths relative to the later wanderings of the Raven after the release of the elements necessary to life on the earth, and particularly those in connection with animals, represent him as always hungry, unscrupulous and deceptive, and friendly only for selfish purposes. In the early spring before the salmon had come into the rivers, or the berries had ripened on the mountain sides, the season of little food, Yehlh happened to be on the seashore near Dry Bay and very hungry. He saw a king salmon jumping in the ocean and he commenced to plan how he could take it, for he had neither canoe, spear, nor line. Going back from the shore he found in a deserted camp a piece of an old cedarbark mat, an old woven spruce root hat, an eagle skin, and a jade adze "tsu-hootar." Putting on the hat, folding the mat about his body, and dressing his hair with eagle down, he took the jade and seating himself on a big boulder at the edge of the water said to the salmon, "Tsu-hootar is calling you bad names, he says that you have an ugly black mouth and that you are afraid to come up to the shore." This so enraged the salmon that he came towards the shore, when Tehlh said, "Wait a little, I have to go to the woods" for he had no club and the salmon must always be killed by striking it on the head with a club. When he returned, he again reviled the salmon and when it came and jumped in shallow water he killed it. He then kindled a fire with his rubbing sticks and prepared the fish for cooking. In the meantime many small birds came around hoping to get something to eat, and the Raven sent them off to gather skunk cabbage leaves to wrap the fish in, but those that they brought he condemned as too small or smelling bad, and told them to go to the far mountain where the proper kind grew. As soon as they had disappeared he wrapped the fish in the discarded leaves, scraped away the fire and the gravel beneath, buried the fish, and covered it with the hot stones and the fire. When the fish was cooked, he ate all of it and collecting the bones, carefully wrapped them in the old leaves and covered them with the fire and when the little birds returned with the mountain leaves he showed them the bones, saying that the fire had eaten the flesh. Then all of the birds felt very badly, the little chickadee cried bitterly and continually wiping its eyes with its feet wore away the feathers which ever after showed a white stripe from the corners down. The blue jay was so angry that he tied up the feathers on top of his head which have ever since formed a crest, for when the Tlingit are angry they tie the front hair up in a knot; while the robin in his grief sat too close to the fire and burned his breast red.

Tluke-ass-a-Gars

The carved post on the left of the ornamental screen was named Tluke-ass-a-Gars "Wood-worm Post" and illustrated a very important happening in the early life of the family that is believed to have caused the separation of the body that first migrated northward. The large upper figure represents Ka-kutch-an, "the girl who fondled the wood-worm," which she holds in front of her body with both hands. Over her head are two wood-worms whose heads form her ears. Beneath is shown a frog in the bill of a crane. The whole post symbolizes the tree in which the wood-worm lives, the crane lights on the outer surface and the frog lives underneath among the roots.

It is said that in early days in a village that would seem to have been near Klawak, on the west coast of Prince of Wales Island, there was a chief of the Tlow-on-we-ga-dee family whose wife was of the Kon-nuh-ta-di. They had a daughter just reaching womanhood. One day after the members of the household had returned from gathering firewood, the daughter, picking up a piece of bark found a wood-worm which she wrapped up in her blanket and carried in the house. After the evening meal she took it into the back compartment and offered it some food, but it would not eat, and then she gave it her breast and it grew very rapidly and she became very fond of it, as if it were her child, and as time went on her whole life seemed to be absorbed by her pet which she kept secreted. Her constant abstraction and absences grew so noticeable that the mother's suspicions were aroused and one day she detected her fondling the worm that had now grown as large as a person. She called the chief and they wondered greatly for no one had ever seen anything like it. As she played with the worm she sang to it all the time:—

"Da-a-a see-ok bus k-e-e-e.	Tchi-ok kon nok
They have small faces.	Sit down here.
Tu usk-k ka tel kin ka	Tchi-ok kon nok
They have small fat cheeks.	Sit down here."

The father told the uncle and he sent for his niece and set food before her, and while she ate he stole away to see the worm, which she had hidden behind the food chests in the back apartment. That evening the uncle called the people together and told them that his niece had a great "living creature" Kutze-ce-te-ut that might in time kill them all and they decided to kill the worm. Another reason given for the destruction of the creature was that it was held accountable for the loss of much food that had been mysteriously disappearing from the grease boxes for some time past.

The following day the aunt invited her to come and sew her martin skin robe, and in her absence the men sharpened their long wooden spears and going to the house killed the worm. Upon her return she cried bitterly and said they had killed her child and she sang her song night and day until she died. Then her family left this place and migrated north. In commemoration of this event the Tlow-on-we-ga-du family display the tail of the worm on their dance dress, pipes, etc., as they attacked that part, while the Kon-nuh-ta-di display the whole worm figure as they killed the head which was the most important part.

Objects Associated With the House

Closely associated with the "Whale House," and in the keeping of the chief, were many ceremonial objects in crest form, that were never exhibited except upon such important occasions as when the whole family was assembled and much property was distributed to those of the opposite phratry who had assisted at house and grave building, cremation, etc. Most prominent among these was a great wood feast dish, and an exceptionally large basket. The former was known as Thluke-hotsick "wood-worm dish," and as a crest object it told the same story as the carved interior post previously described. It was hollowed out of a tree trunk 14 feet 6 inches long, 2 feet 6 inches wide and 1 foot high. It was shaped and ornamentally carved and painted to represent a wood-worm and inlaid along the rounded upper edge with opercula. In 1885 it had so far decayed that its usefulness was past although it was still displayed upon ceremonial occasions (Fig. 6).

The basket although at least two generations old, has been carefully cared for so that it is in an excellent state of preservation. It is named Kuhk-claw "basket mother" on account of its great size, measuring 33 inches in both height and diameter. It was woven of split spruce root in cylindrical form, by a woman of the family, in the characteristic weave of the Chilkat, where alternate spirals of woof are in the double twining and plaiting, giving a rough and irregular appearance to the wall surface. The only variation on the outside are four short darker colored lines of weave which mark its capacity at different heights as we mark a commercial measure. It is fitted with twisted root handle for carriage. Both of these receptacles were used at feasts, filled with native food, and are generally known throughout southeastern Alaska.

Fig. 6. Wood-worm Dish, as seen in the House.

The Present Whale House

In 1899 this house and Yehlh-hit (Raven) House adjoining were torn down and preparations for the erection of new buildings were gotten under way, and in the winter of 1901, after the walls were up and the roof on, a great potlach was given by the Kon-nuh-ta-di, to the three Wolf families of the opposite phratry in the tribe and the Kagwan-tan of Sitka, in which over ten thousand dollars in property, food, and money were distributed. The head chief of the family the master of the whale house Yehlh-guou "Raven's slave," welcomed his guest upon landing, wearing the Raven hat. The new house although modern in form and of two stories took the old name, and it stands today windowless and doorless, the interior grown up in weeds, a monument of the last great potlatch of the Chilkat, as the chief died soon afterwards and his successor has neither the means to finish it nor the desire to live in it and the elaborate carvings have never been placed but are stored and will probably so remain.

PLATE 1.

Decorative figures carved in bas-relief on the face of the retaining timbers supporting the two interior superimposed platforms. For their positions in the house see Fig. 6. The three upper figures represent the native hammered copper plate, "Tinneh," which was an important feature in the ceremonial life of the Northwest Coast and was the most valued of possessions, while that below was said to symbolize "Kee-war-kow," the highest heaven. (See p. 22.)

PLATE 2.

Carved and painted screen at the back of the house partitioning off the chief's apartment. It is called Su-kheen, or "rain wall." The central figure with outstretched arms represents the Rain Spirit, while the small crouching figures in the border are called Su-cou-nutchee, "raindrops splash up," or the splash of falling drops after striking the ground.

A portion of the screen has been broken off and the otherwise unsymmetrical form of the drawing is due to photographic distortion. Its position in the house is indicated by Fig. 6. The hole through the body of the symbolic figure is the door or entrance to the apartment behind. (See p. 23.)

THE WHALE HOUSE OF THE CHILKAT

PLATE 3.

a) Carved interior post to the right of the entrance, Gonakatate-Gars, representing the mythical sea monster that brings good fortune to one who sees it and illustrates a story in the early wanderings of Yehlh, the Raven. At the top is "Gonakatate's child" who holds a hawk in its paws. Next is the head of "Gonakatate," the principal figure whose body extends to the bottom of the post. He holds in front of him a whale, peeping from whose blow hole is the head of the Raven. On the back of the whale is the figure of a woman. (See p. 25.)

b) Carved interior post to the left of the entrance, Duck-Toolh-Gars representing the legendary hero, "Black-Skins" rending the sealion. The large human figure is Duck-Toolh, who holds a sealion by the hind flippers. The head at the base of the post represents the island upon which he stood while tearing the sealion asunder. (See p. 26.)

PLATE 4.

THE WHALE HOUSE OF THE CHILKAT

a) Carved interior post to the right of the decorative screen in the rear of the house, Yehlh-Gars, Raven Post, telling the story of the Raven capturing the king salmon. The main figure with head at the top represents the Raven, holding the head of Tsu-hootar, or "jade adze," and standing upon the head of a fish. From the mouth of Raven is issuing a bird representing lies. (See p. 28.)

b) Carved interior post to the left of the decorative screen in the rear of the house, Tluke-ass-a-Gars, illustrating the story of the girl and the wood-worm. The human figure above is that of Ka-kutch-an, "the girl who fondled the wood-worm." She holds the wood-worm in front in her hands. Two worms are peeping around her head. The lower figure represents a crane holding a frog in its bill. (See p. 29.)

In the Time That Was

Dedicated to
Ah-Koo

Done into English by
J. Frederic Thorne
(Kitchakahaech)

Illustrated by
Judson T. Sergeant
(To-u-sucka)

Being a volume of Legends
of the tribe of Alaskan Indians
known as the Chilkats—
of the Klingats

As told by Zachook the "Bear"
to Kitchakahaech the "Raven"

In the Time That Was

"And There Was Light."

Zachook of the Chilkats told me these tales of The Time That Was. But before the telling, he of the Northland and I of the Southland had travelled many a mile with dog-team, snowshoes, and canoe.

If the stories suffer in the telling, as suffer they must afar from that wondrous Alaskan background of mountain and forest, glacier and river, wrenched from the setting of campfires and trail, and divorced from the soft gutturals and halting throat notes in which they have been handed down from generation to generation of Chilkat and Chilkoot, blame not Zachook, who told them to me, and forbear to blame me who tell them to you as best I may in this stiff English tongue. They were many months in the telling and many weary miles have I had to carry them in my memory pack.

I had lost count of the hours, lost count of the days that at best are marked by little change between darkness and dawn in the Northland winter, until I knew not how long I had lain there in my blanket of snow, waiting for the lingering feet of that dawdler, Death, to put an end to my sufferings.

Some hours, or days, or years before I had been pushing along the trail to the coast, thinking little where I placed my feet and much of the eating that lay at Dalton Post House; and of other things thousands of miles from this bleak waste, where men exist in the hope of ultimate living, with kaleidoscope death by their side; other things that had to do with women's faces, bills of fare from which bacon and beans were rigidly excluded, and comforts of the flesh that some day I again might enjoy.

IN THE TIME THAT WAS

Then, as if to mock me, teach me the folly of allowing even my thoughts to wander from her cold face, the Northland meted swift punishment. The packed snow of the trail beneath my feet gave way, there was a sharp click of steel meeting steel, and a shooting pain that ran from heel to head. For a moment I was sick and giddy from the shock and sudden pain, then, loosening the pack from my shoulders, fell to digging the snow with my mittened hands away from what, even before I uncovered it, I knew to be a bear trap that had bitten deep into my ankle and held it in vise clutch. Roundly I cursed at the worse than fool who had set bear trap in man trail, as I tore and tugged to free myself. As well might I have tried to wrench apart the jaws of its intended victim.

Weakened at last by my efforts and the excruciating pain I lay back upon the snow. A short rest, and again I pulled feebly at the steel teeth, until my hands were bleeding and my brain swirling.

How long I struggled blindly, viciously, like a trapped beaver, I do not know, though I have an indistinct memory of reaching for my knife to emulate his sometime method of escape. But with the first flakes of falling snow came a delicious, contentful langour, deadening the pain, soothing the weariness of my muscles, calming the tempest of my thoughts and fears, and lulling me gently to sleep to the music of an old song crooned by the breeze among the trees.

When I awoke it was with that queer feeling of foreign surroundings we sometimes experience, and the snow, the forest, the pain in my leg, my own being, were as strange as the crackling fire, the warm blanket that wrapped me, and the Indian who bent over me smiling into my half opened eyes.

So were our trails joined and made one; Zachook of the Northland, and I of the Southland, by him later called Kitchakahaech, because my tongue moved as moved our feet on the trail, unceasingly. And because of this same love of speech in me, and the limp I bore for memory of the bear trap, for these and possibly other reasons, and that a man must have a family to bear his sins, of the Raven was I christened by Zachook, the Bear, and to the family of the Raven was I joined.

Orator among his people though he was, Zachook was no spendthrift of speech. But surly he never was; his silence was a pleasant silence, a companionable interchange of unspoken thoughts. Nor did he need words as I needed them, his eyes, his hands, his wordless lips could convey whole volumes of meaning, with lights and shades beyond the power that prisons thought. Not often did he speak at length, even to me, unless, as it came to be, he was moved by some hap or mishap of camp or trail to tell of the doings of that arch rascal, Yaeethl, the raven, God, Bird, and Scamp. And when, sitting over the fire, or with steering paddle in hand, he did open the gates that lead to the land of legend, he seemed but to listen and repeat the words of Kahn, the fire spirit, who stands between the Northland and death, or of Klingat-on-ootke, God of the Waters, whose words seemed to glisten on the dripping paddle.

So it was upon an evening in the time when we had come to be as sons of the same mother, when we shared pack and blanket and grub alike, and were known, each to the other, for the men we were. We had finished our supper of salmon baked in the coals, crisply fried young grouse and the omnipresent sourdough bread, and with the content that comes of well filled stomachs were seated with the fire between us, Zachook studying the glowing embers, I with that friend of solitude, my pipe, murmuring peacefully in response to my puffing.

As usual, I had been talking, and my words had run upon the trail of the raven, whose hoarse call floated up to us from the river. Idly I had spoken, and disparagingly, until Zachook half smilingly, half earnestly quoted:

"He who fires in the air without aim may hit a friend."

And as I relapsed into silence added: "It is time, Kitchakahaech, that you heard of the head of your family, this same Yaeethl, the raven. Then will you have other words for him, though, when you have heard, it will be for you to speak them as a friend speaks or as an enemy. Of both has Yaeethl many."

I accepted the rebuke in silence, for Zachook's trail was longer then mine by many years, and he had seen and done things which were yet as thoughts with me.

For the time of the smoking and refilling of my pipe Zachook was silent, then with eyes gazing deep into the fire, began:

"Before there was a North or South, when Time was not, Klingatona-Kla, the Earth Mother, was blind, and all the world was dark. No man had seen the sun, moon, or stars, for they were kept hidden by Yakootsekaya-ka, the Wise Man. Locked in a great chest were they, in a chest that stood in the corner of the lodge of the Wise Man, in Tskekowani, the place that always was and ever will be. Carefully were they guarded, many locks had the chest, curious, secret locks, beyond the fingers of a thief. To outwit the cunning of Yaeethl were the locks made. Yaeethl the God, Yaeethl the Raven, Yaeethl the Great Thief, of whom the Wise Man was most afraid.

"The Earth Mother needed light that her eyes might be opened, that she might bear children and escape the disgrace of her barrenness. To Yaeethl the Clever, Yaeethl the Cunning, went Klingatona-Kla, weeping, and of the Raven begged aid. And Yaeethl took pity on her and promised that she should have Kayah, the Light, to father her children.

"Many times had Yaeethl, because of his promise, tried to steal the Worlds of Light, and as many times had he failed. But with each attempt his desire grew, grew until it filled his belly and his brain.

"Was he not Yaeethl, the Great White Raven, the Father of Thieves? What if the Wise Man put new and heavier locks upon the chest after each attempt? Were locks greater than the cunning of the Raven?

"Now Yakootsekaya-ka, the Wise Man, and his wife had a daughter. Of their marriage was she, a young girl, beautiful and good. No man had ever seen her face. On no one, god or man, had the eyes of the young girl ever rested, save only her father and mother, the Wise Ones. Ye-see-et, a virgin, was she.

"Yaeethl, of his wisdom knowing that the weakness of men is the strength of children, that a babe may enter where a warrior may not cast his shadow, bethought him of this virgin, this daughter of Yakootsekaya-ka. As the thought and its children made camp in his brain Yaeethl spread wide his snow-white wings.

"Thrice he circled high in air, then took flight towards Tskekowani, the meeting place of Memory and Hope. Like Chunet, the

Arrow, he flew, straight, and as Heen, the River, swift. Twice ten moons, and another, flew Yaeethl without rest of wing before he drew near the cabin of the Wise Man. Away from the lodge he alighted, by the edge of the spring were his white wings folded, by the spring where the daughter of the Wise Man would come for water.

"Then, with the power that was his, Yaeethl, the God, changed the shape that was his, the shape of the raven; into a small white pebble did he change, and lay in the water of the spring, and in the water waited for the coming of the girl.

"Long waited Yaeethl, the Pebble, with the patience of wisdom and great desire. And the girl came.

"Beautiful in her maidenhood, graceful in the dawning of her womanhood, came the girl, the virgin, the daughter of Yakootsekaya-ka, the Keeper of the Worlds of Light. Stooping, she dipped her cup into the cool water. From the edge of the spring rolled Yaeethl, into the cup he rolled, and lay quiet in the shadow of her hand. Quiet he lay, but full of the Great Desire.

"And the girl saw him not.

"To the lodge returned the maiden, bearing the cup, the water, and the Pebble. Into the lodge entered the maiden. In the lodge where lay the Sun, Moon, and Stars, was Yaeethl.

"From the cup the Wise Man drank, but Yaeethl moved not. From the cup the Mother drank, and Yaeethl was motionless. When the Daughter raised the cup to her lips, toward her lips rolled Yaeethl. Softly he rolled, but the Mother, ever careful, heard the sound of the pebble on the cup-side, and the keen eyes of the Father saw the white pebble shine.

"'Do not drink, Daughter,' said the Wise Man, laying his hand on the maiden's arm. 'Small things sometimes contain great evils. A white pebble it may be, and only a white pebble. Yaeethl it may be, Yaeethl the Raven, Yaeethl the Father of Thieves.'

IN THE TIME THAT WAS

"Then the Mother took the cup and out through the door cast the water. Through the door cast the pebble. And when the door of the lodge was closed behind him Yaeethl, the Disappointed, once more took his own form, the shape of the raven, white of wing and white of feather.

"Back to earth flew Yaeethl, angry, ashamed, but more than ever filled with a great longing for the Worlds of Light that lay locked in the chest of the Wise Man.

"Klingatona-Kla, Earth Mother, wept long and sore when empty-handed returned Yaeethl, loud she wailed, making sure she must remain forever dark and barren. But Yaeethl, the Undaunted, comforted her with strong words, and renewed his promise that the Light should be given her in marriage, and her disgrace forgotten in many children, children should she have as the shore has sand.

"Though he had flown as speeds Hoon, the North Wind, the going and coming of Yaeethl had eaten three winters and two summers.

"Awhile he rested in the lap of Klingatona-Kla, for the winter he rested, but with the coming of the spring, he spread again his wings and took flight towards the lodge of the Wise Man, towards the Great Desire. Mightily he flew, and swift, for though the dead make the journey between the opening and the closing of an eye, for the living it is a long trail.

"When again he alighted, wing weary, by the spring where the daughter of Yakootsekaya-ka drew water, Yaeethl remembered the shape and whiteness that had betrayed him, remembered the traitor Pebble, and from the memory gathered wisdom.

"Close to his side folded he the wings of whiteness, beneath his feathers tucked head and feet, and grew small. Small and yet smaller he grew, as melts ice before the fire, and when the shrinking was ended he had taken upon himself the form of Thlay-oo, the sand grain. As Thlay-oo, the Little, he waited.

"As Thlay-oo, the Invisible, watched Yaeethl for the coming of the maiden. Waited as does the bear for the coming of Takeete, the After Winter. Watched as does the lynx for the young caribou.

"And as before came the girl, cup in hand, innocent in her maidenhood, wise in her womanhood, in both beautiful. Gracefully she stooped and filled the cup with the water of the spring. Into the cup floated Yaeethl in the shape of Thlay-oo. In the spring water he sank and lay against the bottom of the cup. Small was Yaeethl, but big with desire for what was within the chest of the Wise Man.

"Then the lodge door opened and received the maiden and the cup, received Yaeethl the Grain of Sand, Yaeethl the Raven.

"To Yakootsekaya-ka, her father, the girl gave the cup, and the Wise Man drank of the water. Drank, but saw not Yaeethl, the Invisible. To the wife, her mother, the maiden gave the cup, and of the water the Mother drank. Drank, but heard not Yaeethl, the Still. Then the maiden, Ye-see-et, the Virgin, daughter of Yakootsekaya-ka, the Keeper of the Sun, Moon, and Stars, lifted the cup to her lips.

"The Mother spoke not. The Father moved not. The Daughter drank.

"Past the red of her lips, by the white of her teeth, down the throat of the girl rolled the grain of sand. Rolled until it lay close under her heart, and paused. Under the heart of the maiden lay Yaeethl, waited Yaeethl, grew Yaeethl. Warmed by the heart of the maiden Yaeethl grew.

"And time passed.

"Then the mother of the maiden, looking upon her daughter, became troubled in her mind. Troubled was the mind of the Mother, but silent her tongue.

"And time passed.

IN THE TIME THAT WAS

"Again the Mother looked upon her daughter, and looking, spoke to the Wise Man, her husband, of the thought that was hers. Spoke she of the troubled thought concerning the maiden, their daughter.

"When the Mother's thought was the thought of the Father his heart was filled with anger at his daughter for the disgrace she would bring upon his name. Angrily he questioned her, that he might revenge himself upon the thief of her innocence. But the girl looked into the eyes of her father and denied both thief and theft. No man had she seen save him, her father. Of the cause of The Thought that troubled them was she ignorant, and as innocent as ignorant. And the truth shone from her eyes as she spoke, straight was her tongue. Empty of shame was her face.

"And the Mother, looking into the eyes of her daughter, believed. And after a time was the Wise Man convinced. Yet troubled were they and lost upon the trail of thoughts. Tender had they always been of their daughter. Ten times as gentle were they now, for Yaeethl lay big under the heart of the girl, though they knew him not, and of their love was she in sore need.

"And time passed.

"Then upon the maiden came Kod-se-tee, the Woman Pain, and Yaeethl entered the lodge.

"Yaeethl whom they knew not, Yaeethl the Boy in the maiden's arms. Tokanay, the Baby, they called him, with love-light in their eyes they named him. Strong and large grew he quickly. So quickly grew he that the maiden and her mother were in a valley between the mountain of pride and the mountain of wonder. And in the Wise Man's heart flowed a great river of love for Tokanay the Beautiful, Tokanay the Swift Growing. In the hands of the Boy were the three hearts held.

Their eyes and their thoughts were filled with him, so that room for other things there was not. So was the locked chest and its contents forgotten.

"Then on a day, a day of days to the Three, the Boy spoke his first word.

"'Kakoon.'

"Kakoon, the Sun, was the word, and 'Kakoon, Kakoon, Kakoon,' said the boy, crying and stretching his arms toward the chest in the corner of the lodge.

"The Wise Man listened and laughing said: 'He would take my place as Keeper of the Worlds of Light.' Then because his heart was so soft with love that he could refuse the Boy nothing, Yakootsekaya-ka undid the many curious locks and fastenings of the great chest and took out the Sun.

"Kakoon, the Sun, he took and gave it to the Boy wherewith to play. And the Boy ceased his crying when the Sun was in his hands, laughing as he rolled the Yellow World about the floor of the lodge. All day did the Three watch him with loving eyes.

"On the next day the Sun lay in a corner of the lodge, unheeded by the Boy. A new word had he learned:

"'Dis-s.'

"Dis-s, the Moon, was the second word, and as before, 'Dis-s, Dis-s,' cried the Boy.

"Proudly and lovingly the Wise Man laughed, saying: 'Surely is he eager to take my place.' And from the moving of the love in his heart that answered to the cry of the Boy as arrow to bowstring, Yakootsekaya-ka unfastened the strong and heavy locks of the chest and into the hands of the Boy gave the Moon for plaything. Of Dis-s, the Moon, made he plaything for the Boy. And for that day were the Boy's cries hushed as he spun and tumbled the White World on the lodge floor. And his laughter was music to the ears of the Three.

"But the next day the Moon lay with the Sun. In the corner they lay and the Boy looked not at them. Another word was his cry, a new word.

"'Takhonaha."

"Takhonaha, the Stars, was the cry of the Boy, and again, to comfort him, the Wise Man opened the great chest, and from it poured the Stars into the lap of the Boy, poured the chest empty of the Worlds of

IN THE TIME THAT WAS

Light. And the Boy laughed loud. Laughed until the Wise Man, the Wife, and the Maiden, his mother, laughed that he laughed, as he dripped the bright stars through his fingers, dripped the waterfall of stars. Then the Wise Man questioned as he laughed: 'What shall he cry for tomorrow? And what shall we give him, the Unsatisfied, now that the chest is empty?'

"And the Boy laughed.

"Night came, and the Wise Man, and his Wife, and the Maiden-Mother, their daughter, slept. With Tokanay, the Baby, in the hollow of her arm slept the girl.

"As they slept, from the hollow of the arm of the maiden there crept a raven, Yaeethl the Raven, Yaeethl the Snow-White, Yaeethl the Father of Thieves.

"Softly crept he, with many times turned head and watchful eye on the Three, sleeping. To the corner where the Boy, careless, had dropped the Shining Worlds, to the corner by the open, empty chest crept Yaeethl the Noiseless.

"And the Three slept.

"Beneath his right wing hid Yaeethl the Sun. Beneath his left wing hid he the Moon. Within his claws gathered he the Stars.

"Asleep were the Three.

"The lodge door was closed, locked was the door of Yakootsekaya-ka, Keeper of the Worlds of Light. Fastened tight were the windows. Barred were door and windows to keep out Yaeethl, the Thief. For a moment stood Yaeethl, turning his head to find some hole through which he might escape, then toward the wide chimney he flew.

"Still slept the Three.

"Wide spread were the wings of Yaeethl, the Flying, and the great light of the Sun was uncovered. Brightly it shone, straight into the eyes of the Wise Man gleamed the fierce light.

"Awake was Yakootsekaya-ka, crying: 'Yaeethl! Yaeethl! 'Tis Yaeethl! Awake!'

"Awake was the Wife and the Daughter, and the Three strove to catch the Raven, the White One. But the great light of the Sun was in their eyes and they were blinded so they fell in each other's way. And in the throat of the chimney was Yaeethl, flying upward.

"Then did the Wise Man call upon Kahn, his sister's son, Kahn, the God of Fire, to aid him. Up blazed Kahn and tried to catch Yaeethl, the Fleeing, in his red teeth, but near the top of the chimney was Yaeethl, so that the teeth of Kahn could not reach him.

"Then Kahn called upon the Wise Man to blow, and the Wise Man puffed out his cheeks and blew with full lungs, and by his blowing Kahn stretched high his long black arms and tightly curled them about the White Raven.

"Then did Yaeethl, the Strong of Wing, struggle mightily. Against Kahn, the Fire God, did he struggle, beating with his white wings. Long did they struggle, until from the lungs of the Wise Man was the breath gone, and the arms of the Fire God, the smoke arms, grew thin and weak.

"With his wings beat Yaeethl, breaking the hold of the smoke arms, Yaeethl the Free, Yaeethl the Ever Black One.

"Forever were the wings and feathers of the Raven blackened by the smoke arms of Kahn, the God of Fire.

"Back toward Klingatona-Kla, the Earth Mother, the Barren, flew Yaeethl holding tight the Sun, Moon, and Stars. But after him came the Wise Man, full of anger. And the Shining Worlds grew heavy. Heavy was the pack of Yaeethl, and weary his wings. Afar off was Klingatona-Kla.

"Then did Yaeethl, the Pursued, Yaeethl the Heavy Laden, cast from him Kakoon, the Sun. To the east threw he the Sun, and flew on.

IN THE TIME THAT WAS

"Again did the Wise Man come close behind, and again did Yaeethl ease his burden. From him threw he Dis-s, the Moon. To the West cast he the Moon.

"Then was Yakootsekaya-ka left behind for a time, but the Raven weary and burdened, flew slowly, and once again he felt the breath of the Wise Man ruffle his feathers. No time had Yaeethl to stop, on nothing could he rest.

"Opened he his claws and scattered wide the Stars. To North and South fell Takhonaha, the Stars, to East and West fell they.

"Then was the promise of Yaeethl fulfilled. Thus kept he his word to the Earth Mother, and gave her light, that she might see. Gave her Kayah, the Light, to father her children and wipe out the disgrace of her barrenness. And the children of Klingatona-Kla were as the sands of the sea.

"But upon Yaeethl, the Raven, had fallen the curses of the Wise Man. Three curses: Blackness, Hoarseness, and the Keeping of One Shape. And as his feathers were blackened, so, thereafter, was his heart darkened with eternal selfishness."

I was silent. My pipe had gone out, and Zachook was bent low over the dying fire. I was thinking of another story of a Child who had given Light to the World, and suffered for the bringing.

The Water Carrier

"When You Give a Potlach,
Forget Not He Who Carries the Water."

Thank Yaeethl for that," said Zachook as I rose with dripping beard from the stream where I had drunk deep, with many sighs of satisfaction and relief. "His pack is not heavy with thanks of men these days."

"Thank the Raven? For what?"

"The starving man asks not the name of the owner of the cache, but his heart is filled with gratitude."

"That may be, but no cache of Yaeethl's is in this stream."

"The ignorant deny all they cannot see."

"Wise sayings feed neither fire nor belly," I retorted, provoked by the criticism of my companion, thinly veiled behind his customary proverbs, and attempting to pay him in his own coin from my slender store of Klingat adages. "'Only a beggar gives thanks.' Is it not your teaching that he who gives in this world receives the benefit, since in Tskekowani[1] his possessions shall be as his gifts here? If Yaeethl wants my thanks, if they are the due of the Raven, he has them, but why or for what I know not. Your words are like the ice of a windy day, rough and cloudy."

"You are right, Cousin. I forget at times that you are only a white man. Let me touch thy ear with my tongue."

---

[1] The next world.

IN THE TIME THAT WAS

"Cha-auk.[2] In the Time before Time, there was no water upon the earth or in the bowl of the sea, and Shanagoose the Sky gave neither rain nor snow.

"In one place only was Heen, the water. In a deep well it was, the father of wells, hidden among the mountains that lie between here and Tskekowani.

"To Heenhadowa, the Thirst Spirit, belonged the well, by Heenhadowa was it guarded. By the door of the well-house sat he by day, in front of the well-house door was his bed by night. And none might enter.

"Never did he leave the well, morning, noon or night. From the water he took life, to the water he gave life. To no man, woman, or child, to neither animal nor bird, to nothing that walks, creeps, or flies would Heenhadowa give of the precious water. Not so much as would moisten the tongue of Ta-ka the Mosquito would he give, though men died.

"To quench their thirst men chewed the roots of young trees and the stalk of Yan-a-ate.[3]

---

[2] Ages ago.
[3] Species of wild celery.

"A few men there were, brave of heart and moose-legged, who had travelled the weary journey to the well among the mountains, the mountains marked with the trail of Oonah, the Gray One, Death, seeking the water that is life.

"And of them?

"Is it not well said that Oonah, Death, and Koo-stay, Life, are brothers, and he who seeks one finds the other?

"And Heenhadowa laughed, first at their black lips, later at their white bones, and drank deep but gave not.

"Now Yaeethl, the Raven, Desirer of All Things, longed most for those that were forbidden, concealed, or like the favor of women, not to be had for the asking. And since the water was denied, his tongue ached with dryness, and Yan-a-ate lost its savor. Also was his heart moved by the prayers of men and the cries of women. But his tongue troubled him more than did his heart, his tongue and his cupidity, so that he was moved to try his cunning where the strength and bravery of men had failed.

"No crooked trail through forests and over mountains had Yaeethl to measure with his feet, but on his wings of blackness was he borne straight to the place of the well.

"Well and well-house he found, found also Heenhadowa, watchful, moving not from his place. As one greets an old friend new found spoke Yaeethl to the Thirst Spirit. With smooth tongue and soft words spoke the Raven, claiming kinship through the cousin of his grandmother's grandmother. Said also that when he left his father's country he was bidden seek that old and true friend of the family, Heenhadowa the Wise, the Generous Giver of Water. As bidden, so had he obeyed and flown straight without halt or rest to bow before his mighty relative, and taste of his wonderful well, the like of which not even his father had, who possessed all things.

"But the Maker of Thirst laughed at the Raven and mocked him, bidding him, if he would drink, find or dig a well of his own.

"Again Yaeethl recounted their connected lineage, from mother to mother's mother, from family to family and tribe to tribe, tied with proof and argument, lashed with meek bows, and smoothed with soft flattery.

"Heenhadowa laughed scornfully, cast from him the claim of cousinship, and mocked at Yaeethl's tongue, dry from the dust of many words.

IN THE TIME THAT WAS

"Then Yaeethl drew about him the parka of anger and answered scorn with scorn, mockery with mockery, and laughter with laughter.

"In his father's country, said Yaeethl, they gave the name of Heenhadowa to mangy dogs and unclean women. Glad was the heart of Yaeethl that the Thirst Spirit denied the relationship he had laid as a snare, the denial would make his father proud. As for the well, 'twas now known to the most stupid, even to men, that it was but an empty hole in the ground, covered by the well-house to hide the dryness thereof, and no deeper than Kaelt-tay, the Seagull, scratches in the sand for nesting.

"Laughed Heenhadowa again, saying that belief or unbelief of Raven or man lessened not his treasure by a drop.

"Then Yaeethl's words flared as firesparks. Hot words of evil sounding names, vile as only the brain of Yaeethl could fashion, taunts that bit and stung festeringly like the nettles of Sech-ut,[4] names that would disgrace the family of a Siwash, callings that would make even a squaw-man hang his head in shame. Can I say more of the bitterness of the tongue of Yaeethl?

"Heenhadowa laughed.

"To battle Yaeethl challenged the Thirst Spirit: 'Come forth and meet me, you fatherless son of a shameless mother, littering of a slave's slave.

"'Come with me to the plain below and I will make of thy blood another well, for another of thy family of dogs to guard.'

"Flatteries and arguments, insults and challenges fell into the same echoless hole, bringing to Yaeethl only the laughter of Heenhadowa and increase of thirst.

"Then was the heart of Yaeethl heavy within him, but not so heavy as his face said, for it is not the way of the Raven to eat quickly of discouragement, though he turned and left the well and its guardian like a gambler who has lost his last blanket.

"Not far did he go. Only so far as to be hidden from the eyes of Heenhadowa, where silence might mother the children of his brain. And since the brain of the Raven is full of the seeds of cunning a plan was quickly born.

---

[4] Devil's Club.

"Back toward the well flew Yaeethl, but, since he who sees the tail of a lone wolf imagines the whole pack, he alighted at a distance where the eyes of Heenhadowa saw as one sees in a fog. A space the size a man uses for his lodge he cleared of all bushes and weeds, to the smallest blade of grass he cleared it of everything that grew.

"When the space was as the palm of a man's hand the Raven spread his wings until every feather showed and, first bowing low to Hoon-nach, Yunda-haech, Sa-nach, and Deckta-haech,[5] who guard the four corners of the earth, walked slowly around the sides three times, at every third step stopping and making strange motions and stranger sounds, as does an Icht[6] when he would drive the evil spirits away.

"From each corner he took a stone and spat upon it and cast it over his shoulder, and in the dust drew the shapes of animals like unto rolled deer-thongs, animals with two tongues such as no man has seen upon earth.[7]

"To the space Yaeethl dragged logs and laid them end across end and bottom on top. As each tier was laid he sang words in a strange language, and as he sang, spat upon and cast pebbles over his shoulder as before.

"But toward Heenhadowa were the eyes and tongue of Yaeethl the eyes of the blind and the tongue of the dumb. Busily he worked and loudly sang his charms, but to the Thirst Spirit he gave neither look nor word.

"On Yaeethl were the eyes of Heenhadowa fastened, strained were his eyes, watching the doings of the Raven, wide his ears to catch the words of the songs and charms.

"When the roof was on and the house finished to the last piece of moss between the logs, Yaeethl again circled it three times, bowed again to the guardians of the earth's ends, and without looking behind, entered the lodge and closed the door.

"Curiosity filled eyes and ears, heart and belly of Heenhadowa. Though he had lived since the Beginning, never before had he seen what that day he had seen, never had his ears been greeted with such words and songs.

---

[5] North, East, South and West.
[6] Witch Doctor.
[7] Snakes are unknown in Alaska.

IN THE TIME THAT WAS

"And to Heenhadowa the inside of the lodge was the pack, as was the outside the lone wolf tail.

"Even so had Yaeethl planned, nor was that the end of the cunning of the Raven, who knew that no door can bar the going in of curiosity.

"Long sat Heenhadowa before the door of his well-house, gazing at the lodge of Yaeethl. And the longer he sat and the longer he gazed the keener grew his desire to see what was hidden from his eyes by the walls and closed door, grew until it tortured him as the thirsty are tortured, beyond endurance.

"And Heenhadowa rose from his seat by the well.

"From the place where he had sat for ages rose the Thirst Spirit and stepped softly. Toward the closed door he moved as moves one who is pulled at the end of a thong, for the fear of the unknown was upon him. But stronger than his fear was his desire to know what lay behind the door, stronger even than his fear of those strange animals that were drawn in the dust, dust pictures that made his blood ice.

"Before the door he stopped and glanced back the way he had come, at his well and well-house he looked, then pushing against the door with his hand, stepped within the house builded by Yaeethl, made by Yaeethl the Raven, Yaeethl the Cunning.

"No man knows what Heenhadowa found within the lodge of the Raven. Only this we know.

"When the time of the boiling of a salmon had passed, from the door stepped Yaeethl walking as a man walks who has been carrying a heavy pack. Behind him he closed the door and against it rolled a heavy stone, a stone so heavy that not even K'hoots the Grizzly, the Strong One, could have moved it away again.

"Within the lodge was silence, silence big with unborn noise.

"To the well of Heenhadowa, the father of wells among the mountains, the well untasted of man or beast, flew Yaeethl, Yaeethl the Desirer of All Things.

"And when the Raven stood beside the well he bowed his head and drank.

"Some say that it took him many moons, some put it the length of a man's life, but, long time or short time, when the head of Yaeethl the Raven was lifted the well was dry.

"Of water there was none in the well of Heenhadowa.

"In the belly and mouth of the Raven was the water. All.

"Then did Yaeethl spread wide his wings of blackness and fly the way of his coming.

"As he flew over the bosom of Klingatona-Kla, the Earth Mother, in this place and in that he spat out some of the water. And where spat the Raven there sprang up streams, and rivers, and lakes.

"When he had flown so long and so far that the water was gone from his mouth, and in his belly was not fresh, then from his belly and his mouth he cast it, salt, and Athlch, the Ocean, was."

I waited silently, for there was an uplift in Zachook's voice that made me think there was more to follow, but it was only:

"If you listen to the words of them that know not, they will tell you that Haechlt is a great bird the falling of whose eyelids makes thunder, the flashing of whose eye is the lightning, but if my words be the words of truth, then is thunder the angry voice of Heenhadowa whom Yaeethl made prisoner, and lightning the cracks in the lodge

IN THE TIME THAT WAS

walls when he throws himself against them, struggling to be free. Should he succeed——

"But, bird or Thirst Spirit, from Yaeethl is the gift of water. So say I again——when you drink, give thanks to the Raven that chewed roots are not the answer to thy dry lips,—give thanks, and pray that the rock rolls not away."

And I gave thanks, quoting to myself another of Zachook's sayings, "Better a wasted arrow than lost game."

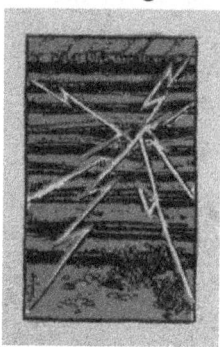

Ta-ka the Mosquito and Khandatagoot the Woodpecker

"As Foolish as One Who Shoots Arrows at Mosquitoes."

Zachook, with a half amused, half sympathetic smile at my futile efforts to slaughter a small percentage of the mosquito cloud that enveloped us, made a smudge of leaves, and I willingly exchanged the tortures of being eaten alive for those of slow strangulation in the acrid smoke.

My remarks had been neither calm nor patient, consisting mainly of my entire vocabulary of opprobrious adjectives and epithets several times repeated and diversified, aided by a wide, but wholly inadequate, range of profanity in the various languages at my command. And, to digress slightly, I would recommend the study of Arabic and Spanish to those feeling a similar need; they do not meet all requirements of forcible expression, but they add some wonderful flights of imagination to the more practical English expletives.

Zachook was apparently as unimpressed as the mosquitoes, but when I had recovered some portion of my breath and equanimity, remarked: "He who shoots with his tongue should be careful of his aim."

Choking with anger and smoke I could only splutter in reply, while Zachook continued:

"Ta-ka is Ta-ka, and Yaeethl is Yaeethl."

"What has the Raven to do with these insufferable pests? Has he not enough to answer for without linking his name with these suckers of blood? Yaeethl is Yaeethl, but Ta-ka is Ta-ka."

IN THE TIME THAT WAS

"Yaeethl or Ta-ka. The get of the Raven are ravens, and from Yaeethl comes Ta-ka the Biter.

"When the selfishness of men had driven the gods from the earth, the Great Ones held a council in Tskekowani, a potlach in the World Beyond. All the gods were there. They talked of the sins of men and of the punishments that should be visited upon them. Long they talked.

"Then Theunghow, Chief of Gods, called each by name, and bade him name his sending.

"And each god named a sickness, a pain, or a killing.

"At one side stood Oonah the Death Shadow, and in his hand held his quiver. And as each punishment was named, into his quiver placed Oonah an arrow, sharp-pointed, swift-flying, death-carrying.

"The quiver was full, and all had spoken, all save Yaeethl the Raven, who by the cook pot sat smiling, eating.

"To Yaeethl spoke K'hoots the Grizzly, saying:

"'Dost thou send nothing, Brother? Behold, the Quiver of Death is full, and from the Raven is there no arrow of punishment for men. What arrow gives Yaeethl?'

"'Why bother me when I am eating? Is there not time after the pot is empty? Many arrows there are. Because men insult me shall gods spoil my eating?' Thus spoke the Raven as he scraped the pot.

"Then Hckt the Frog urged, saying:

"'Art thou a god, or is thy belly a god, that in the council the Raven takes no part?'

"'A god am I, and a god have I been since the Beginning, thou son of wind and slime. But that my ears may be no longer troubled, a little punishment will I send, that the sons of men forget me not. No arrow from Yaeethl shall find place in Oonah's quiver. Arrow and messenger both will I send. Thy punishments carry the peace of death, mine the torment of life.'

"'And this punishment of thine?' asked Hckt, sneering.

"And Yaeethl, as from the pot he cleaned the last morsel, replied:

"'Ta-ka.'

"Of all the punishments named by the gods, the first to reach the earth was that of Yaeethl,—Ta-ka the Mosquito.

"To Khandatagoot the Woodpecker, the simple-minded, went Ta-ka, and from the Woodpecker claimed hospitality. And the rights of a stranger gave Khandatagoot to Ta-ka, gave him a place by the fire, and of his food a share, for his head a shelter, treating him as the son of a sister is treated. Together they fished and hunted, together they ate and slept. Of the hunting and fishing the chief part was Khandatagoot's, of the eating and sleeping Ta-ka's, Ta-ka who from Yaeethl came.

"On a morning the Woodpecker fixed his canoe, and alone to the hunt went the Mosquito.

IN THE TIME THAT WAS

"All day was Ta-ka gone. Low hung the sun when to camp he returned. Slow flying came the Mosquito, and as blood is red, so was the body of Ta-ka, and swelled mightily.

"Then was the Woodpecker frightened, thinking his friend wounded, and crying, ran to help him. To the ground sank Ta-ka, but no wound could Khandatagoot find.

"Many questions asked the Woodpecker, and to them Ta-ka replied:

"'No hurt have I, but full is my belly, full of the choicest eating that ever made potlach. Yet much did I leave behind, the feasting of many months did I leave.'

"Then was the belly of Khandatagoot pinched with hunger for this good eating, and of Ta-ka claimed his share.

"On the tongue of the Woodpecker placed Ta-ka a drop, saying: 'No more can I give of what I have eaten, but as you have shared with me, so shall I share with you. The fill of many bellies is there left.'

"'Where is this sweet eating?' asked Khandatagoot, 'Tell me the trail that I too may feast until my wings are heavy.'

"'No trail is there, Brother. The red juice of a dead tree is this eating, a dead tree in the forest. It's name I know not, but hunt, and you shall find it. Go quickly, lest others get there first.'"

"And since then," said Zachook, throwing another handful of leaves on the fire, "since then the Woodpecker spends his days seeking in dead trees the red juice that flows in the veins of live men."

Also from Benediction Books ...
Wandering Between Two Worlds: Essays on Faith and Art
Anita Mathias
Benediction Books, 2007
152 pages
ISBN: 0955373700

Available from www.amazon.com, www.amazon.co.uk

In these wide-ranging lyrical essays, Anita Mathias writes, in lush, lovely prose, of her naughty Catholic childhood in Jamshedpur, India; her large, eccentric family in Mangalore, a sea-coast town converted by the Portuguese in the sixteenth century; her rebellion and atheism as a teenager in her Himalayan boarding school, run by German missionary nuns, St. Mary's Convent, Nainital; and her abrupt religious conversion after which she entered Mother Teresa's convent in Calcutta as a novice. Later rich, elegant essays explore the dualities of her life as a writer, mother, and Christian in the United States-- Domesticity and Art, Writing and Prayer, and the experience of being "an alien and stranger" as an immigrant in America, sensing the need for roots.

About the Author

Anita Mathias is the author of *Wandering Between Two Worlds: Essays on Faith and Art.* She has a B.A. and M.A. in English from Somerville College, Oxford University, and an M.A. in Creative Writing from the Ohio State University, USA. Anita won a National Endowment of the Arts fellowship in Creative Nonfiction in 1997. She lives in Oxford, England with her husband, Roy, and her daughters, Zoe and Irene.

Visit Anita's website
 http://www.anitamathias.com,
and Anita's blog
 http://dreamingbeneaththespires.blogspot.com, (Dreaming Beneath the Spires).

The Church That Had Too Much
Anita Mathias
Benediction Books, 2010
52 pages
ISBN: 9781849026567

Available from www.amazon.com, www.amazon.co.uk

The Church That Had Too Much was very well-intentioned. She wanted to love God, she wanted to love people, but she was both hampered by her muchness and the abundance of her possessions, and beset by ambition, power struggles and snobbery. Read about the surprising way The Church That Had Too Much began to resolve her problems in this deceptively simple and enchanting fable.

About the Author

Anita Mathias is the author of *Wandering Between Two Worlds: Essays on Faith and Art.* She has a B.A. and M.A. in English from Somerville College, Oxford University, and an M.A. in Creative Writing from the Ohio State University, USA. Anita won a National Endowment of the Arts fellowship in Creative Nonfiction in 1997. She lives in Oxford, England with her husband, Roy, and her daughters, Zoe and Irene.

Visit Anita's website
   http://www.anitamathias.com,
and Anita's blog
   http://dreamingbeneaththespires.blogspot.com (Dreaming Beneath the Spires).

www.ingramcontent.com/pod-product-compliance
Lightning Source LLC
LaVergne TN
LVHW041205250326
834689LV00001BA/15